Hide and Seek: A Journey to Life

By Sheree Baldwin- Muhammad

Dear Reader,

First of all, I would like to thank God for bringing me through life's trials. The many obstacles I have faced have shaped and molded me into the person that I am today. Although some circumstances were not pleasant, I would not have changed anything.

I would like to dedicate this book to my mom and my 4 children, who suffered at times due to my own insanity. Thank you for loving me through it all. I would also like to thank Bishop Jay Ramirez, Pastor Fran Malafronte and my best friend Quamay Alves for being my personal counselors. I don't think I would have made it through without your wisdom, guidance and encouragement.

The events in this book are of a sensitive nature, but I chose to share them with you. This book started out as a collection of poems that I wrote over the past 10 years. It was through writing that I developed a deep understanding of myself and more importantly, my personal relationship with God.

Hide and Seek: A Journey to Life is a collection of poems and narrative that tells the story of overcoming the trauma of rape, depression and domestic violence.

Thank you for purchasing my book. I hope it touches your heart and helps you find peace in the midst of your own personal journey to life.

Sheree Baldwin-Muhammad

Table of Contents

Chapter 1

The Beginning

I don't even know where to begin. There have been so many things that have happened in my life. I have been told by many, "Girl, I don't know how you made it alive and sane..."

Sanity is only what one perceives one to be looking from the outside. But on the inside, memories plague me every day; voices trying to tell me to give up. But there is a HIGHER Voice that keeps ringing in my heart telling me... I have brought you this far... and that is what keeps me going...

I have come too far
to turn back now.
To make the wrong decisions
would be detrimental to my life,
spiritually and emotionally.
Shall I be consumed in thought???
or shall I press on??
Regardless of how I may feel,
knowing that God is in control of all things.
Even when I fail to make the right decisions
or choose the wrong path
He is still there to help me
to retrace my steps.
He sets me back on the path of righteousness.

I have come too far
to allow my emotions to take control
clouding my judgment.

I must stay focused on the goals set before me.
I press on regardless of how things may appear
I must walk and have no fear
for God is with me;
even in the midst of the storm.

Shall I be overtaken by the winds of life that blow
or shall I stand???
Unshakeable
Unmovable
planted firmly in who You have called me to be.
Even when I can not clearly,
I must heed Your call
to step out in faith
and trust YOU
above all else.

I have come too far
to wallow in pain,
feelings of guilt and shame.
Never to regret
but learn from my mistakes...
and move on...
But at what cost???
I am not sure...
What am I willing to give
or give up
in order to achieve the goals set before me?
Am I willing to Trust YOU?

Reflecting on the past,
I see the error of my ways.
Do I choose to repeat them
again...

and again...
Decisions...

I am yet at another crossroad in life.
Should I go or should I stay?
Should I fight or should I walk away?
For the battle is not mine,
it is the Lord's.
I must walk according to His timing,
and not my own..
What cost would I pay to follow my own way?

I have come too far
to be set back,
making a decision I might regret..
Speaking words that man can never forget.
Making a wrong turn could cost me my life,
so I proceed with caution...
Because I have come too Far
to turn back..

Turn back to what, you may ask?

My life has been a spiral of emotions which all trace back to my childhood.

We lived in the "little white house with the white picket fence" some would say; Mommy, Daddy, my little brother and I.

As you can see I subconsciously put "mommy" first. That is because "daddy" was out of the picture by the time I turned 8. Looking back he had checked out far before then.

I remember prancing in front of him, asking,

"Daddy, do you like my dress? Do you think I am pretty?"

Only to be shushed and pushed aside for the *Eyewitness News* or some other television program. I longed for his attention, but he just couldn't see me… the little girl standing before him crying out to be loved.

Do you even see me?
Standing there,
desiring to be the apple of your eye,
your pride and joy?
The princess...
No more.
This little girl desiring
A father's love.
Neglected and shoved aside.
How often I've tried to hide
my true feelings.
This little girl crying out
Silent tears unheard
Longing to be held
you left a void,
an emptiness inside.
Trying to suppress the pain,
As I called out your name
But no one heard me.
Daddy

Chapter 2

What's Love Got to Do with "IT"?

To be loved…But what is love?

I had never truly experienced what some say is the basis of all relationships. The love of a dad for his little girl was something I never felt, experienced, or was able to grasp.

So began my spiral, my quest to find this missing piece…

LOVE….trying to fill it at any cost. I gave of myself to try to get what I thought would fill the void of needing love and acceptance from my father.

My childhood was filled with promiscuity, experimentation with trying to feel good, to feel loved; it didn't matter as long I got my "fix".

I was introduced to the "feeling" while playing "Hide and Go Get *"IT"*; a perverse form of hide and seek children played back in the day.

The first time *"IT"* was introduced to me was at the age of 10, I was not quite sure what *"IT"* was, but I was glad to have friends. A bunch of kids moved in across the street. They would come over to my house and "play" because my brother and I were never allowed to leave the yard.

Tag you're *"It"*!

Never did I know
The true meaning of the game.
Was I supposed to run?
Was I supposed to hide?
And what if they find me?
Do I give in?
Or will they take me,
and strip me of my innocence
Telling me to hush.
Don't tell a soul!
It won't hurt.
But IT did;
To my core
As I was labeled a whore.
Not by others,
but by myself.

Tag you're It!
I played the game.
I hid the shame.
Never telling a soul
but the game took its toll.
As an addiction rose,
A new lifestyle I chose.
As I continued to play,
But this time…

I was "IT"…

At age 10, I was addicted to sex.

"She's Gotta Have *IT*" had nothing on me. Anything that I could hump or grind, I tried to find; as long as I could get my "fix", I was good. As long as I could feel that sensation that seemed to take away the pain, I gained power in manipulating others to do as I pleased.

At age 13, I was a master of masturbation because finding a partner to participate the way I wanted was becoming slim without being labeled a whore. Even though inwardly, I felt that I was already one. Outwardly people whispered "lies". Never telling me how they felt to my face. They smiled at me and laughed behind my back.

The idea of playing "Hide and Go Get *It*" went out the window as I saw no need to hide. I just went and got "*IT*".

At age 14, I started on a treadmill of "dating"; being with one partner at a time seemed more appealing and even more grown up. I began my never-ending "quest" for LOVE in all the wrong places.
Because of my maturity level by this point, boys did not appeal to me; so I choose to "date" older guys and in many cases men.

My first boyfriend was only a couple years older than me but at age 14, dating an almost 17 year old was not acceptable so I hid behind going roller-skating and spending the night at his cousin's house just to get my "fix".

My first love was only short lived as he was getting his "fix" with a few older girls as well, so it was... On to The Next One and the next, and the next, and the next…I can't even count how many frogs I kissed in search of the *ONE*…

Prince Charming

In my dreams he is there,
riding upon his white horse
seeking to find his fair maiden.
His every waking hour is devoted to finding her,
knowing that she is awaiting his arrival.
She sits in her castle
captivated by thoughts of when he will come,
what he will look like,
whether he would slay a dragon for her
and whisk her away...
Holding the key to her heart.
With one word she will know him
or will she be awaken by true love's kiss...
She sighs as she looks in the mirror
wondering if her beauty will last
or if he will ever find her
locked away in this dungeon called life...

My prince charming...
Romeo, Romeo wherefore art thou Romeo...
One Day my prince will come....
True love awaits...

Chapter 3

Prince Charming?!

In a crowded room,
Our eyes locked
As the boys popped and locked.
Hip Hop took on a new meaning
As I skipped over
Dancing to the beat of his drum.
He had that certain style
The one that makes a girl go wild
And His eyes were on me.
We were one, with just one kiss.
He fulfilled my every wish.
Is this my prince?

"Was *HE* my prince?" I wondered as he walked across the crowded room. He saw me and my pretty dress. He noticed me. It must be him, so I thought as I gave my all to him; spending every waking hour trying to please him.

I felt safe.

After all, my brother and his brother were best friends. His family loved and accepted me. He would walk miles to see me from a town away. I would scrape up just enough change to take the bus to see him. We spent days and nights together; quiet walks on the beach.

He was the ONE! I had found it....

Ideas of marriage filled our heads. He was 18 and I was 16; much too young for all that, so we were told. No more game of Hide and Seek for me, I had found what I was looking for.

So I thought, until I got pregnant, AT 16!

What was I going to do?

I decided to have the baby at first but I was scared.
When I told my mother, my decision started to change.

"You'll never be able to go to college now", were words spoken over me.

"You'll ruin your life!"

"What will THEY think!?"

What will *they* think? ...

I was plagued with the thought of what others would think of me...

This was no prince after all but yet another frog! My mind raced as he rejoiced over the idea of having a baby with me...But is this *really* what I wanted to do?

And what would **THEY** think?

I waited... almost too long according to the doctors at the clinic as I ended one life to save another, **MY OWN**.

I ran from it because I didn't want to see.

I didn't want others to know my little secret. Once again, I was playing Hide and Seek; this time not wanting anyone to find me.

"You Killed My Baby!" echoed in my head when he found out what I had done. These words haunted me for years to come.

I had to break away from this torment I felt inside. Hiding once more, I ran from one arm to another trying to embrace the inner child who was screaming to be released from the inward prison.

Relationship after relationship, I sought to be loved; trying to cover up the wounds, trying to hide the shame, and trying to stop the voices inside my head that were trying to tell me that I was unlovely, unlovable, and unloved.

Chapter 4

A Way of Escape

Graduation Day, June 1986. I saw a way of escape from the "lie" I had been living. Freedom awaited in a land far, far away. Little did I know that you can not run away from your past, if you are still carrying it inside of you. Nevertheless, I left Connecticut to find a better life and to seek PRINCE CHARMING; because obviously he was not in CT!

"Boys, just only want ONE THING", I would say to myself.

Not realizing it was me who only wanted one thing and if that one thing was not fulfilled, I would run in search of something else.

BUT what?

I was still playing the game of Hide and Seek, as I sought a new life. Florida brought a new promise, a new start. I was on my way to becoming a doctor although I was stricken with the thought of "not being good enough".

After all, I wasn't good enough for my daddy to stay with me... and look at all of the boys I *loved* who dumped me for others. I didn't deserve to have anyone love me because of my past, so I gave up the dream and settled for what was easier to attain.

In Florida, I felt free. No one knew me. I thought I had found a way of escape, immersing myself in my studies. I felt a sense of accomplishment as I pressed forward to follow my dream of becoming a doctor.

I wanted to be a pediatrician because I desired to help others. I had volunteered at a hospital during high school and loved working with the children in Pedi. Halfway through my first year, I found that being pre-med was harder than I thought. I looked at my grades and cringed as I downed myself for not being *smart enough.*

My decision to change my major was solidified by my advisor's comment of "you will never make it into med school with grades like this." Immediately I doubted my ability and the words of "you're not good enough" reared its ugly head.

I changed my major to Education. My reasons were not logical at the time, looking back I wish I had pressed on and became Dr. Baldwin but at the time, my self esteem was so low that I had none. I never esteemed myself to be anything more than what people told me I could be and nothing more.

I excelled outwardly, smiling pretty for the cameras to see, but no one knew the torment which lied within.

I walk around with a smile…
I laugh but no one sees the inner pain
of feeling trapped,
not able to breathe…
Conforming to the image that I must portray before man.
Only real to God;
for it is He who really sees the tears I cry.
He is the only one who knows my heart as others pass by.
I give a smile…
a wave…
a hug…
a kiss;

even a word of encouragement..
but who is there when I need them???
It is funny when you give and give;
and then when you have nothing left,
all people ever want is
MORE...
So I paint a picture on a blank canvas..
I smile pretty for the cameras,
for all to see,
hiding what is truly going on inside of me...
because if you could really see..
would you still love me???

Chapter 5

Seek and You Shall Find

So I continued to play the game of Hide and Seek, running away from my past, not wanting anyone to see my insecurities. I sought long enough to catch a glimpse of True Love.

I found "A Man" in a church in Lakeland. A college friend took me there. He was amazed with my beauty, my hair, my complexion. He told me he had never seen a *black* woman that was so beautiful.

He had been raised to be racist in some stick town in Alabama . I was captivated with his flattery enough to follow him to Carpenter's Home Church.

I listened to the message spoken by the preacher which spoke directly to my heart. *This* was the Love I had been searching for.

I gave my life to HIM, confessing Jesus as My Lord and Savior. I cried at the altar and asked for forgiveness for all I had done.

The secret lies.

I begged for Him to take away the pain and take away the shame.

I felt Love for the first time, but I was young and still didn't see my worth in Christ. It was all but a concept, an idea. True revelation of who He was and who I was were yet to be discovered.

Voices still rang in my head, echoes from my past, reminding me of who I was and would never be.
A choice had to be made.

Which way would I go?

In the Midst of the Garden...
There is a tree that is pleasing to the eye...
It's fruit calls out
beckoning me to take and eat...
It is pleasing to everything within my being
and I desire to know,
to touch,
to feel,
to taste of the sweet nectar...
The forbidden fruit fulfilling every lustful desire
knowing no right ~ nor wrong...
but only to satisfy the hunger from within.
Quench this thirst
as I take a bite...
Only to find that the intoxicating aroma
had toxins from which I could not detox myself of.
I was dying a slow death....
Consumed with an insatiable hunger
an appetite that could not be curbed...
The more I ate,
the more I wanted...
after all...

The things that I would...
I do not
and the things that I would not,
I do...
oh wretched ... am I..

or is it me?
or is it this tree?
to which I have connected myself to...
I chop away at the root...
But I can not break free...
Lest someone save me...
~from myself...
As I look and see a man standing
In the midst of the garden...
He calls himself the Vine...
I,
a branch...
That if I abide in Him....
and He abides in me...
I can do all things..
and will have everlasting life...
but apart from him..
I can do nothing...??

I Can do Nothing...

~and That is it what I had done thus far
NOTHING
but attempt to succeed
but fail...
Repeatedly running around in circles
to the point of exhaustion...
only to have the life sucked out of me?

I seek but rarely find
I knock and have the door slammed in my face
By everyone else...

but TO YOU

I surrender!
I give up!

Let me take from this Tree You call The Life...
The Way..
The Truth...

Then what have I lived??..

Death...

Lost within the Lies
Told to me time and time again.
"I love you",
they would say and then walk away.

So give me this cup
and let me drink ...

As I feel new life springing up within me...
flowing like rivers of water...
I am refreshed...
I am renewed...
I Can Do all things..
I am because He is..
and apart from Him..
I can do Nothing...
Well at least No Good thing...

Which tree will you eat?

from In the Midst of the Garden...
The choice is yours...

Choices?

Decisions?

Which way do I go?

I so longed to understand this new found *Love*, but my flesh and my mind would not let me forget who I had been for the past 17 years. My body screamed out to be loved, to be touched, to be embraced.

Could I break free from these desires?

Was it possible to totally follow God's Word and be perfect?

Perfection... a word that I so desired.. but always failed to be. Looking at how Big God was.. and how small I was... I knew that perfection was so far from what I had been, so I hid once more and continued to seek....

Chapter 6

A Wrong Decision, In the Name of Love

On my summer break before my Junior year of college, I visited my newborn niece back in Connecticut. She was a beautiful reminder of what I was missing. Questions rose in my mind of what "Tyree" would have looked like.

Tyree was going to be my baby's name, if I had kept her. I wasn't sure if it was going to be a girl or a boy but Tyree was the name we had picked out. It was a combination of my name and the father's name. He thought of the name when I told him on Father's Day that I was pregnant. He was so proud and commenced to tell everyone that I was going to have his baby. The "girl of his dreams", the *sweet Sheree,* was going to have his baby.

Little did he know that a plot was thickening against that idea and I would choose to "Kill His Baby!"

I was a murderer, but holding my niece gave me comfort.

I rocked her and touched her tiny fingers; God's precious gift.

In the corner of the room lurked a shadow. It caught my eye but faded in the distance. He smiled and introduced himself.

I laughed and said to myself, "Ha, He thinks he's cool!"

He made a declaration that He would make me *his*. I laughed at the thought. I was always the predator, preying on men. This time I would play it smart and cool.

He was smooth; not much to look at but he had that certain swagger. I tried to play hard to get; hiding, inwardly longing to get caught. I played the game of Hide and Seek.

He wined and dined me. He sang his way into my heart. Babyface lyrics still ring in my head:

"I give good love, I'll buy your clothes, I'll cook your dinner too as soon as I get home from work."

The rest of the lyrics had me sold! He promised me the world and delivered it to me on a silver platter. Little did I know that it was a trap of the enemy using my desire to be loved against me. A wolf in sheep's clothing, he professed to be a Christian and even introduced me to his brother who was a pastor.

He is the ONE!
I was caught.

Nothing or no one could tell me any different. I was pampered from head to toe. I had everything I could ask for, including a DIAMOND RING! Yes! He flew to Florida and proposed.

My Prince had come riding not on a horse but a jet plane! But was I the only one?

He had a son and a baby momma. I didn't want to break up a "happy home" like *that* women did that took my daddy away. So I gave the ring back, telling him to work things out with his ex for the baby's sake. I knew she still loved him because she had threatened me several times to stay away from him.

Little did I know why.

Chapter 7

A Big SLAP in the Face

SLAP!

I felt a hand come across my face and found myself on the floor of the hotel room looking up at him.
He threw the ring down at me and said,

"If you ever take that ring off again, I'll Kill you."

He then grabbed me and started rocking me in his arms sobbing,

"I don't know what I would ever do if I lost you. You are my life. I love you so much. I am sorry I hit you. You made me do it. You said you were going to leave me. I'll never do it again."

"He loves me! He must really love me if he is crying like this," I thought to myself.

The sting of the slap became numb. And I accepted the lie and stayed.

He returned to Connecticut, leaving me in Florida to gaze at my ring. I held my hand up so high that my arm almost fell off. I was awestruck by the flower shaped diamond on my left ring finger. He picked it out just for me because I was *his* flower.
Aww, How Sweet, but everyone knows flowers die if not watered.

The ring came with a price. I was now *HIS*. I was no longer my own person, but his property.

When I returned to home, I learned that he had been seeing his ex and I was outraged!

I took off the ring and threw it at him.

Remember the slap in the hotel?

Well that was nothing compared to the beating I got.

One again, he reminded me of the threat of killing me if I took off the ring. Once again he cried, begging my forgiveness, expressing his undying love, and once again I believed him, hiding my bruises. So began a dangerous game of Hide and Seek.

I tried to hide the bruises I received from you.
But the wounds ran deeper than you could ever know.
Never on my face they would show.
I smiled
and laughed
Throughout the years.
Silent tears
stained my pillow.
I wanted no one to know
The secret I held inside
As I tried to hide
Black and Blue.

But no one knew
As I covered up for you.
"I fell"
I would say
After all, I was clumsy.
But no one knew the real me.

Hide and Seek
Trying to find a way of escape
From this nightmare.
I tried to awake
But over and over
These words spake;
"If you leave me.. I will kill you."
But little did you know,
I was already dying
I was Black...

And Blue...

Chapter 8

Senior Year

In December of 1989, my senior year of college, I found out I was pregnant.

AGAIN!?

But this time I was engaged to be married and was in love so what difference would it make.

I was happy and excited to tell my fiancé the good news.

But he was not thrilled. He told me I was trying to trap him. He told me that he already had one child and another would ruin his chances of becoming a star.

He had aspiration of being a big recording artist and my being pregnant was just not in his plans.

ABORTION was NOT an option for me.

Never Again.

Being a Born Again Christian made the decision or even the thought of abortion even more a SIN!

In retrospect, it's funny that I worry about having an abortion being a sin when I had been sinning by having sex outside of marriage. Abortion was the farthest thing from my mind and after pastoral counseling, it was the farthest from his.

I returned to school scared stiff. I thought they were going to kick me out, after all it was a Christian School! Once again I diverted to the old childhood game of Hide and Seek.

I started wearing baggy clothes, sneaking food in my room from the cafeteria, and puking my brains out at night. I read the bible out loud to my belly every night because I had read in one of my Child Development classes that the baby could hear even while in the womb.

I found comfort in the Word for the first time. It was as if God himself was with me in that room. He led me to scriptures to read and through the Holy Spirit I found peace and solitude in just being with HIM. I was in a safe place.

You are My Dwelling Place.
My secret place.
I run and hide in you.
When the world is dark and cold,
I find Life in You.
I find peace in You.
I am because You are...
And apart from You
I can do nothing...

Good thing I didn't have a roommate at the time because by April my belly really was starting to show. Hide and seek, definitely not wanting to get caught for fear of the outcome. But I knew one thing, I could feel His Presence from that moment on. God was working a miracle inside of me in more ways than one.

Graduation was just weeks ahead when I got called to the Dean's Office! My heart raced. I broke out in a cold sweet as I waited to be seen.

Tag, You're It!

I was found.

I was sure he was going to tell me to leave. I sat down in the chair holding my breathe.

"Sheree, it has come to my attention that you may be pregnant." He started.

Ok, this is it!

I thought, four years of college down the drain.

"Yes, I am," I timidly replied.

There was a few seconds pause which felt like an eternity. My heart raced. My palms got sweaty and I could feel the baby flutter in my stomach.

"I am proud of you for staying in school instead of quitting like so many other girls." He added with a smile.

I breathed a sigh of relief.

"Unfortunately," he continued.

OH NO!
Here it comes.
I knew my actions would get me in trouble in the end.
I was sunk.
No degree for me.
And I worked so hard!
How stupid I was to get pregnant again!
I was a loser!
No good.
Look at you now, Sheree.
Your life is ruined.
Voices rang inside my head.

Chapter 9

Voices

These Voices were far too familiar.
Voices that reminded me of what an awful person I really
was. Voices reminding me of my past, my mistakes, and my
failures.

You'll never amount to anything.
Nobody loves you.
Why don't you just kill yourself?

Oh I forgot to tell you that when I was 8, after my father left.

I not only had to deal with my insatiable desire to be loved,
feelings of rejection but also depression.

I forgot to tell you that I would carve "daddy" with a knife on
the bedroom wall and would often turn the knife on myself
never penetrating deep enough to draw enough blood to bleed
to death but the scars remained inwardly, as well as
outwardly.

I cried silent tears.

*If you look close enough you would see
and truly find the real me.
The one hiding behind
the smiles and the laughter...*

*If you looked into my eyes
you would find*

that it leads to the window of my soul.

Silent tears welling up that I try to hide.
The sorrow and pain that I feel inside.
You would see the weariness and distress,
If you only took the time to look deep within.
You would find
That my eyes
are the
window to my soul...

Searching,

seeking,

trying to find
relief from the sorrows left behind.
Memories fill my mind
not often wanting to rewind;
they play over and over.
I try to escape
the emptiness I feel inside.
Reaching out to Jesus
and taking hold of His hand
For I know that He will never leave me...
He loves me
and I trust Him.
But here in this place,
I find no space to rest
from the demands of the day.
So I run away,
hiding the things I would not want others to see.
For if they saw
would they still love me???
So the next time you look in my eyes

look past the mask
I am hiding behind....
to find the real me.
It is easy to see
That my eyes are the window
to my soul...

My soul was broken into a million pieces. The pain was often too much to bear. I wanted to run away. I wanted to hide. I wanted to be loved but it seemed that everyone I tired to love left me.

I must be bad.

I must be punished.

I went on a bought of self hatred.

How could I expect anyone to love me, if I hated myself?

Thoughts of suicide filled my head.

My first attempt was after finding out I was pregnant the first time when I was 16. I figured if I killed myself no one would find out how bad I was. I tried to slash my wrist but not deep enough.

I didn't want to die. I just wanted the pain to stop and the voices to stop telling me that I was a failure.

The second attempt was…

Well let's get back to the Dean's office.

I was sitting there waiting to hear the words "unfortunately you can not stay at this college."

After all it was a Christian college, and I was a Christian. Christians were not supposed to be pregnant out of wedlock.

The dean took a deep breath and said,

"Unfortunately, we may not allow you to walk during graduation. We fear that in your condition you may pass out."

I felt fine. Why were they afraid that I would pass out during graduation?

Liability risk I guess.

Needless to say, I did graduate and I did walk without passing out.

My whole family came down to see me graduate, even my fiance. Well let me back up. Not my "whole family".

My dad didn't bother to come or call. I tried to push away the thoughts, the voice inside my head, and enjoy my day. But they kept haunting me.

My dad was never "there". He never supported me in any important event in my life; not my prom, not my High School graduation, so why did I think he would come now?

He had a new life anyway; so I thought. A new daughter that stole my name; well part of it anyway. My middle name was Lenore and he gave her MY Name! It was bad enough that "That Lady" took my daddy away from *me* when I was 8. But now he had a new daughter and she took MY NAME!

I was replaced as usual.

Lord, take this pain away!

*The feelings of
rejection...
alienation...
humiliation...
leading to depression.*

*Take away the sorrow, the tears, and the fears.
Allow me to rest in Your arms...
for I am Tired.*

*~tired of thinking
~tired of wishing
~tired of hoping
for things
that never seem to come true.*

*Prayers left unanswered...
give me the patience to
WAIT...
~but how long?*

*LORD take the pain away...
I don't want to feel it anymore.
I paint on a smile to hide the tears
and laugh when I want to cry.
Give me the strength to go on...
take the pain away...
what more could I say...
what more could I do...*

I did all I could...

Do I not have
~needs...
~desires...
~dreams...
~hopes...
Let them align with YOURS..
for my own surely fail...
and I am tired of trying
~Take the pain away...

Memories cloud my mind so much,
as my life flashes before my eyes;
as I wait for my name to be called.

Sheree Lenore Baldwin, Bachelor of Science
Deans List 4.0 in Her Major!

"You go girl!"
One of the proudest moments in my life clouded by memories
and voices in my head reminding me of who wasn't there
AGAIN.

I guess my good wasn't good enough.
Perhaps if I was going to med school instead of being
pregnant with a degree in Early Childhood Education, it
would have been to everyone's liking.

Connecticut here I come.

Chapter 10

Back Home..
Home Sweet Home

After returning home, the wedding plans began. After all I couldn't actually have the baby and not be married first, so we pushed the date up to June 7th.

I think.

Much of my life is a fog from here on perhaps from all the blows to the head. Yes, the violence continued and intensified because I was ruining *HIS* life. After all, I was the one pregnant, and getting married to his Crazy *A*… but I was ruining *his* life.

We moved into a duplex with my mom and prepared a room for the baby, My prison. It was where I slept, ate and took care of the new baby. It is where I hid my black eyes, fat lip and bruised face. I was trapped liked a caged rat. I did what I was told. I was his slave. I cooked, I cleaned, and well... *IT* played a big part in our lives.

Waiting 6 weeks was not an option as the doctor told us not to have sex because the likelihood of me getting pregnant again was high. Of course, he was above the law, above what anyone of authority might say and disobeyed every rule, every command and tried to find a scripture to back up his mess. "A woman shall not withhold herself from her husband" was his scripture of choice. And so, pregnancy number 2, well three but who's counting.

If you think he was mad with me for "trapping him" with the first, the second bit of news took him over the edge of RAGE.

After all he was the one who disobeyed the doctor's orders. I was fine with waiting and by that point sex was no longer a pleasure but a form of torture. But he blamed me for getting pregnant again. He threw me down the stairs to make me have a miscarriage. I guess he had seen it on tv but it didn't work. I had to run away from him just to keep my sanity and to save my baby.

I moved in with my mom, who had since moved out because she couldn't stand to see the abuse I endured. I cried day and night. I was at one of the lowest points in my life. I was a mother of an infant less than a year old, and I was pregnant again; married to a maniac. I had nowhere to go, so I hid. But in the game of hide and seek, you are always found.

He chased me down and even came as far as to come to my mother's house to confront me.

How could I leave him?

How would I survive?

I had nothing; I was living in my mom's 1 bedroom apartment.

Should I go home? Or should I leave?

He cried once more, pleading for me to come home. He pledged his undying love and apologized for his action saying, "It would never happen again."

So, I went back.

By this time my husband was "recording" and working full time. He was gone most nights. I prayed each night that the Lord keep me safe from harm. My relationship with God reached new heights.

I hid in Him, seeking Him daily. I had to trust and rely on God like never before. God was truly *with* me… and the new born child I carried within me. Emmanuel, God with me…

Each night he would come home and if the slightest thing was wrong with the house or if dinner was not on the table; SLAP!

I was to keep silent, ask no questions of his whereabouts, after all women were to be seen and not heard. I was to *Obey* my husband at all costs. He was the head and I was, well, the tail. I was under his foot, fist, belt, and any other thing he could grab to hit me with.

I vividly remember one morning. I was nursing my second child on the couch, when he walked into the door. My oldest was playing on the living room floor. I was upset because he had stayed out all night.

I approached him with the question, "Where were you?"

The next thing I knew, the room went black. When I came to, the baby was crying on my lap and my oldest was trying to punch and kick his dad to keep him away from me.

He was only about 16 months at the time; but my oldest son was ready to fight this 180 lb man to keep him off me. The fight continued in the kitchen as I tried to do what I rarely did, which was fight back.

The worst beatings I ever got were when I fought back. He would only grow even more enraged and out of control when I tried to fight back. I have a ringing in my ear to this day from blows to the head from fighting back.

He would "black out" and go wild, punching me like we were in a Mike Tyson fight. I slowly began to learn that if I just played dead. He would stop. I lost the will to survive. I merely existed.

Chapter 11

Existing

Who is this person I see?
It surely isn't me.
And where did my smile go?
Do I dare let my feelings show?
Emotions seared,
I am trapped.
Afraid to run.
Afraid to hide.
I am lost.
Please set me free
From this bondage.
There has to be an answer
To the questions that lie within my heart.
How did this all start?
I often wonder
if life is worth living.
I am dying a slow death.
Do it quickly;
Kill me!
What reason do I have to live?
What more do I have to give?
For I am only
Existing.

We tried year after year to make things work.

We tried counseling.

We tried therapy.

Our marriage was filled with pain. And I often wondered if God was punishing me for killing one of his children long ago.

Was I to suffer for my past?

Is this the price I had to pay?

The pastor tried to reassure me that it was not but messages pointed to 'your sin finding you out' and I was sure that I was found.

I lived a slow death. Seeking God for answers. I felt like He didn't hear me...Voices inside my head tried to reassure me of my greatest fears.

Nobody loved me anyway... How could they? I just have to put up with the life I am living and accept it.

In addition to the abuse, he started cheating on me with various women. He stayed out late almost every night and would often sleep at his cousin's house, just to not have to hear my mouth. I was torn with emotions of wanting him to be home with me, not to have him leave me too.

And what about the kids? I didn't want my children to be without a father like me and have to feel the pain I felt. I often prayed he would never return but eventually he did.

We hardly spoke to each other by this point. I did my business of raising the boys in a comatose state. He sheltered me from all outside influence. The only place I could go was to church and even there I was imprisoned by the views of his family. I tried to be the best Christian and wife I could be.

I went about doing my chores and wifely duties. "No" was never an option. I was his sex slave. I had to do what he desired, when he wanted "*It*"...

And if I declined, he took it, forcing himself on me.

"A wife can not withhold herself from her husband!" he would tell me.

I would lie there lifeless as he rammed himself inside of me breaking the condom in two. I didn't even discover that he used a condom until 2 days later, when it fell in the toilet. He didn't want any more kids. But the broken condom, proved that they were not 100% fool proof. Three month later, I went to the doctor with the fear of finding out I was pregnant with his third child, a girl this time!

Not again was the thought going through both of our heads. We could hardly make ends meet with the two boys we had and he was constantly losing his temper and his jobs. But this time it was a girl. His face lit up with the idea. He had 3 boys already and there was only two girls in the family at the time. He was excited about finally having a girl and inwardly I was relieved that he was *happy* for a change.

Chapter 12

All Good Things Come to An End....

Having a girl was a turning point in our relationship. He stayed home more often, went to church more often, and the violence decreased. He seemed to be a little more content. He came home singing. I began to like him.

I thought he was happy because he was beginning to not dread being married any more. Perhaps he *really* did love me. I had a spark of hope left in my heart which was slowly quenched by the idea that he was seeing another women; but how?

People started telling me about this other women but I didn't believe it. Until one day I started going through his phone records and through his pockets and finding telephone numbers.

I remember doing a reverse lookup on the computer to get the address of one women he was seeing. I drove to her address and whose car was in front?

HIS!

I began throwing rocks at the window and screaming his name. I called his cell but he would not answer. Finally he looked out of the window and told me to go home.

Go Home?!

Me?

Go home? What about him? He was up there with God knows who and I was to go home with 3 babies and just deal with it.

I had gotten tired of the lies.
I was tired of the games.
I wanted to know who she was
and I wanted to know NOW!

I keyed his car and ran away. This time I was going to leave for good.

I had had enough of the abuse.

My mother and I moved into a 4 bedroom house in Fairfield. I worked two jobs and I vowed to never go back.

Chapter 13

Please Baby, Please!

I lived on my own for almost two years. I was about to file for a divorce, when he called. He was living with his cousin and she didn't want him to stay there anymore.

What was I to do? After all, he was my husband.

My mom was outraged that I moved him back into the house. I didn't care about anything but trying to get my family back. I heard that he had gone to jail for attacking his girlfriend. He didn't stay in long but he had nowhere else to go.

He begged me to take him back.

My daughter was two by this time and needed her daddy in her life. How could I deprive her from what I so longed to have?

I never wanted her to feel abandoned by her daddy like I did.

He found a house for us to live in and we moved out. One big happy family, I thought. He was back. No more interference from other people. We continued to go to counseling and surrounded ourselves with family. We had family functions and I would watch the kids while he and his cousin went to the casino. Everything seemed perfect. I got my dose of baby time while watching his cousin's kids and my niece.

All of my kids were walking by now and I had no more babies. My daughter was turning 5 and I had plans on getting my teacher's certificate in order to start teaching full time.

We were living a comfortable life and hadn't moved for almost three years; which was unusual because previously we either got evicted or moved in the middle of the night to avoid getting kicked out. All was great until I went to the doctor for my yearly checkup:

"DID YOU KNOW YOU WERE PREGNANT?"

NOOOOO! NOT AGAIN!?

What about my plans to get my teacher's certification?

What now?

I was afraid to tell their father, my mother, or anyone that I was pregnant again.

Chapter 14

Here, We Go AGAIN!

Not again?

This time the violence picked up again. He threatened to cut the baby out of me. He absolutely did not want me to have another child especially since our youngest was 5.

I wasn't crazy about the idea either. We had just gotten back together and I was finally trying to get my career started.

I had been dependant on him for years. He had held over my head that I would never amount to anything or be anything. I believed him and stayed enduring the pain for almost 10 years. I only was allowed to work part time in various daycare facilities. I worked my way up as far as I could go up the early childhood ladder. I was currently acting director at a daycare in Stamford. Having a baby was not exactly on my agenda either. And having a baby with *HIM* was the last thing I wanted to do. But all he could think of was how could I do this to *him* again?

He insisted on me having an abortion. The word ABORTION left a bad taste in my mouth still after all these years. I still felt the sting of killing my first child and I wasn't about to kill another baby. I had to do something because his anger was growing out of control.

I ran away.

But this time I ran into the arms of the Lord…

I stayed at his brother, the pastor's house. He and his wife prayed over me and read scriptures to me. I found peace and refuge away from him. I surrounded myself with the Word. It was peaceful there.

It was quiet most of the day when the family was away but at night there was murmuring. He tried to call and they hid me. It was there that I sang praises to God, wrote poetry and rested until I was strong enough to leave... or rather until his sisters told me that I had no business being at their brother's house, that I needed to go home to my husband.

So I went home but continued to find refuge in God. I continued to pray. I had to in order to survive what happened next.

Chapter 15

The Secret

After giving birth to my son, life took on some type of normalcy. I went back to work, the kids went to school and my husband; well he came and went as he pleased.

I remember strange calls in the middle of the night from his cousin. She had a one year old who was rather sickly. He would have asthma attacks frequently at night and had to go to the hospital. She would call in the middle of the night for my husband to come down to the hospital. I got angry because he would often leave me and my newborn to tend to this woman and her child. I often would ask him why she didn't call his daddy. He gave me some excuse that he was not around and that he was just helping out his cousin.

One Thanksgiving I remember having the whole family over. He brought a whole house full of new furniture to impress his family. He even cooked to make sure that everything was just perfect; as if I could not cook well enough for *HIS* family.

I remember his cousin coming over with her baby. I took one look at him and said, "Dang y'all family genes are so strong... That baby looks just like you!"

I turned and looked at him. He was looking down at this point. Little did I know why he looked down when I made that statement; but I was soon to find out.

The phone calls in the middle of the night from his cousin continued until one day an argument between them ensued. I knew that tone all too well. He stormed out of the house. He came back in a cold sweat, huffing and puffing.

I asked him what was the matter? He said nothing but I knew it was something.

It was Sunday so I went to church as usual, but alone this time.

I remember the anointing was high. People were speaking in tongues, praying and crying out to God. I began to cry, tears streaming down my face.

Service ended and my mother and I left for home. I remember her mumbling something to the affect of everything will be ok and mentioning something about his cousin's baby.

I am not sure what happened next because it seemed like my life was going in slow motion.

The baby is his? Is all I remember thinking.

The Baby IS His!

Anger welled up inside as all of the days I stayed home watching her kids while they went to the casino flashed before my eyes. All of the days he spent the night over his cousins house to get away from me after an argument.

He was gone when I got home. I waited at the house for him to return. When he got there he asked me about going to a picnic at a mutual friend's house. I held this secret inside all night.

Chapter 16

Memorial Day

It was Memorial Day weekend. Everyone was having fun at the picnic but me. I paced the floor, smiled to cover the pain and laughed asking God why?

There is one question
that is so hard to answer.
So hard to understand
when in the midst of tears,
you seek to find the reason
why???

Although you may quite well be aware.
Seeking for one
who will truly cares
to erase the pain felt inside
when often you just want to run and hide
because the answer you received
is not the one you wished to hear.
So you just ask
why???

Wanting to know the answer.
Will it even make
anything better?
Will it soothe the pain?
Will knowledge of the truth set you free...?
When it comes to matters of the heart...
I think the question should be
why not..
You already know the answer before you ask
The clues were already laid out

but you chose not to listen
but instead
you wonder why???

Why could not things go the way I desired...
Why could you not be who I longed for you to be...
Why does this emptiness not go away?
As I search to find
not the reasons to why...
but WHY NOT!

Why was I not ever good enough for him?
Why did he lie and cheat?
And now, why did he sleep with his cousin?

The truth was about to be known even though deep inside I
had already known the truth for quite some time. I knew the
truth the first time I laid eyes on the boy.

He looked just like my husband. He looked more like him
than my own kids. There was no denying that was his child.

It was getting late and I couldn't wait any longer to confront
him with the question that had been burning in me all day. I
could no longer hide behind a lie.

I sat down on the couch and asked calmly, " Do you have
something to tell me?"

He said, "No."

I leaned in closer looking him directly in his eye, " Do you
have something to tell me?"

He squirmed in his seat. He sensed that I knew something. He had learned from the past that I had some type of insight; intuition. I was able to read him. The Holy Spirit would even go as far as give me scriptures which would read his mail. So he knew not to play with me much by now.

By my tone he knew I meant business. Instead of confessing he got enraged. Yelling and storming around the house but never really answering my question until he broke down crying.

"She was going to tell the whole family. She was trying to "blackmail" me and ruin me. I told her not to say anything. No one had to find out."

Just then I knew the truth. I wanted so much for this to be a lie. But it was true.

"Her baby is yours?!" I asked.

He couldn't speak but just looked at me.

I am not sure what happened next. The rest of the night was a blur.

All I remember is that I was in bed and I heard a clicking noise. I knew he kept his gun under the bed in a gray metal case. I found it one day while cleaning.

He was leaning over the side of the bed. I heard a noise and he rolled over.

I ran into the bathroom.

He ran after me, banging on the door with the gun.

I begged him to be quiet because the kids were asleep. My daughter's room was right across from the bathroom. He said he was going to kick down the door down if I didn't open it. For fear of him waking the kids, I opened the door.

He grabbed me by the hair and dragged me down the stairs. He scrambled around the kitchen for the keys and dragged me outside to his red Maxima.

We drove it seemed for hours with him pointing the gun in my face. I tried to remain calm as my heart raced and I prayed under my breathe in tongues.

"Where are we going?" I asked.

"I can't live with what I have done. I can't. Everybody will know! Everybody will hate me. I can't live with this. And neither will you. Neither will she! I am going to kill you, her, and then kill myself." He sobbed.

I knew that if I got hysterical at this point. We all would be dead. I had to stay calm and figure out a way to get this gun out of his hand and get home safely.

But how?

I tried to reason with him but he kept telling me to shut up.

My prayer got louder and I remember my voice changing. I had to let the Power of God take over like never before. God had to do it because if not, I would be dead.

"If you do this, the kids won't have their mothers or their father," I stated in a calm voice.

He stopped and looked at me as if he was looking through me or saw a ghost.

He sniffed, "But you will leave me. No one will ever have you. I have to kill you."

He continued to look at me as I pleaded for him to put the gun down.

I reassured him that I would not leave; that we would talk in the morning and figure out how to work this all out.

He started the car.

By this time, we had been sitting in the parking lot of his cousin's apartment building. He drove home and climbed in bed.

I checked on the kids who had been left alone during this whole ordeal but they were fast asleep. I said a final prayer as he yelled for me to come into the room. I laid there stiff as a board as he held me close to him sobbing about how sorry he was.
He said he didn't know what he would do if I left him.

He cried himself to sleep.

All the while, I was plotting my escape.

Chapter 17

The Final Escape

For almost 10 years I had been running; playing hide and seek, trying to get away from this man. Beating after beating, I returned partly because I didn't feel I could make it on my own. In addition, I never wanted my children to suffer like I had with not having my dad in my life. It never dawned on me that witnessing abuse was more damaging in many aspects than not having their dad at home. The cycle had to stop but how?

Over the past 10 years, I had built up enough spiritual muscle to stand up for myself. I still had self esteem issues but I knew that God didn't want this life for his daughter.

I have no words to speak...
I sit here in silence trying to understand...
but no words come to mind..
or even a thought to find...
no emotions...
no tears...
no fears...
I have nothing to say and that speaks volumes...
because in the past I would have been a mess
but I have grown I guess
or I have grown tired...
because I have no words..
no thoughts...
no emotions...

I am not moved by the irrational display...
I am just sitting here...
awake after drifting off to sleep for some time...

Wondering..
Caring..
but not moved...
no tears...
no emotions...
I have grown...
Because I knew a time
when I would hv thrown a fit...
ranted and raved..
screamed and hollered..
but now...
I just sit...
praying for you...
Because I once loved you...
but no longer am I there...
My emotions once ran wild...
but God..
But...
God

He came in and calmed the sea...
He placed a new heart within me...
I can now look on you with compassion...
not be riddled with guilt...
questioning
or second guessing..
no tears
no fears..
just concerned...
not worrying about how it affects me...
Loving you enough to let you deal with..
what you need to deal with...
so that either the bond can be strengthened
or broken...
I am good either way...

But I have to leave…
No turning back
I am numb…
void of emotion
no words…
no tears..
no fears..

I am Free…

The next morning I woke up. I decided to leave but I knew I had to do so subtly. I had to pretend to stay but leave. I woke up as usual and got the baby ready to go with me to work. I got the older kids up and ready for school. I said a prayer over them because the usual routine was that he took them to school or to the bus stop. I left the three oldest behind with him. I prayed for their safety as I walked out the door for the last time.

As I drove to Stamford, I began to sob. I wondered if I did the right thing by leaving the older kids home. I wondered what he would do to them if he knew I was plotting my escape. I trusted God to keep them safe.

I was an emotional wreck. There was no way I could go to work like this. I telephoned my mom and informed her about what had happened and asked her to get the kids from school. I telephone my boss, who was a Christian woman and friend, who had gone through domestic violence issues before. She told me to drive straight to her house in NY.

When I got there I told her the story of what had happened. She asked me if I had gone to the police.

The police?

That was the farthest thing from my mind. I had remembered my experiences with going to the police. They were not pleasant. They often questioned me and joked and made fun of the issues stating,

"Well, I see no marks." or "Well, a wife's duty is to have sex with her husband. I see no crime in him wanting sex from you."

They laughed and dismissed the charges. Why would I feel safe going to them for help now, especially a day after the incident? It would be my story against his.

My boss convinced me to go back and file a complaint against him and as well as a restraint order. The ride home seemed like an eternity. I drove to the police station and breathed a sigh as I opened the door.

"Next" yelled the clerk behind the glass.

"Yes? May I help you?"

I froze. I didn't know what to say. Tears welled up in my eyes. I tried to tell them what had happened but my words were all jumbled. They told me to wait there and they would get a detective to talk to me.

They took me into a room and sat me down. They gave me a cup of water to drink and asked me to slowly tell them what happened. I began to tell them the story. They wrote down my statement and asked me why did I wait a day to come down to the station. I told them that I was scared. They told me to go downtown and file a restraint order. I was afraid for my life by this point. I was sure he knew I had escaped.

Chapter 18

Hide and Seek

By this time I really was playing the game of Hide and Seek for my life. The cops told me because he had a gun they would look for him and pick him up. They told me unless they found the gun on him that they couldn't hold him for long and they asked me if I wanted to press charges.

Of course I wanted to press charges! After all he had done to me. After all of the pain he has cause throughout the years. After all the times he hit me. After all the times he cheated on me. After this last incident and the gun. He threatened to kill me! Of course I wanted to press charges.

I remember every time I saw a red Maxima my heart jumped. It was him, I was sure looking for me. I would duck inside buildings and hide. I would hide behind bushes and wait for the car to go by. I was sure he was looking for me now. God help me if he found me!

God help me.

The more I hid from him, the more I sought God.

No matter what today brings
I will trust you...
No matter how hard it may seems
I know you will make a way out of no way...
No matter the disappointments...
I know you have the Master plan...
My life is not my own...

I walk according to your ways...
I trust in your Word...
and know that your promises are true...
No matter what today brings..
I keep this in mind...
and even when sorrow comes
Joy is right there beside me to comfort me...
no matter what....

Chapter 19

My Past Comes to Haunt

Onward I pressed with my life. He had been arrested and had been given only 8 months for possession of the gun. It was his story against mine as far as the attempted murder charges and his slick lawyers got him off.

I felt a new freedom in Christ! I tried to remain at my old church but being among his family members only brought back bad memories in addition to the fact that many of them felt like I made up the gun story and were mad at me for going to the police. I couldn't allow my past to hold me captive anymore so I left to find a new church, a new life.

There was still one empty place in my heart now and that was my undying desire to be loved. I knew God loved me and that I was grateful for it. But to have a man love me, that was what I longed for.

I began to search on the internet in my free time. I felt safe behind the computer because I could be someone else besides this abused and damaged person I saw when I looked in the mirror. No one had to know who I really was unless I told them.

ReeRee was my screen name. I loved the attention of the men from the single sites. The one thing I missed about being married was having sex whenever I wanted. Now the thought of being celibate was not my cup of tea. I wanted so much to please God but my body was screaming out for more.

I started to have sex chats with my cyber friends in the middle of the night while the kids were asleep. I even went as far as to buy a video camera to record myself masturbating and to view men doing the same. My past came back to haunt me as my appetite for sex increased.

I sang in the choir, worked in the children's ministry, and worked on the church drama team by day and by night I was Reeree.

I hid this secret from everyone except the ones reading this now going yeah I remember phone chats with Reeree.

I confused love with lust and felt secure in all the men who professed how much they loved me. One man from Texas caught my eye back then. We had a lot in common, especially the addiction to sex. But Texas was so far away. I wanted someone closer to home. Someone I could touch and feel and...well you get the picture.

Chapter 20

Rekindling Old Love

My internet quest continued until one day I spotted a familiar face but the name didn't match. I decided to send him a note. He replied and I was right it was my old boyfriend from back when I was 16, my first baby's daddy; well it would have been the first had I not had an abortion. He looked good all grown up and he was single!

He invited me to his mother's house for Thanksgiving. It was great seeing all of the family. They all were glad to see me. They told me that they never accepted any of the other girls that he would bring by the house because they just didn't compare to me. Wow what a compliment! I was flattered. They were glad I was back in his life.

Back in his life?

Was I? Back in his life?

Did I want to be back in his life after all he called me every year of the anniversary of the "death" of his child to remind me of Tyree. He lost track of me once I went to school in Florida but the date still haunted me and I could hear his words loud and clear each time the thought of abortion came to mind. Did I want to have to look him in the eye and relive this for the rest of my life?

Yes, I said the rest of my life because by New Years we were contemplating marriage. Our justification was that we were grown now and no one could tell us no, like when we were young. In my heart I felt that it was too soon after my separation from the kids' father. After all it had only been 8 months since I left and I still had to deal with the fear of when he got out of jail. What would he say or do knowing that another man would be raising his kids. He had already warned me of such things when I threatened to leave other times. I knew that he would not be happy with my idea of getting remarried and I really didn't care but it was a concern in the back of my mind.

We felt that God had given us back to each other and given us another chance to have Tyree. One small problem was that my tubes were tied after my last son. The doctor said that they would come unraveled with time and we prayed that if it was meant to be, we would have Tyree.

By February my divorce was final and I was engaged to be married again.

As expected their father hit the fan. He wanted his kids to have no part of this new man in my life and made my life a living Hell.

Chapter 21

History Repeats Itself

I was already dealing with a different hell by now anyway.

My new fiancé seemed to have a problem with women on the computer. I had stopped all of my dealing with Mr. Texas and every other man I had been "seeing" but my new fiancé seemed to like to sneak on the computer at night and chat with these women. He also called them from his cell phone. I confronted him with my suspicions but he denied them all. He told me that they were just friends and I had nothing to worry about.

I believed him at first until his job called one day while he was "out of town on business". They were wondering where he was because he had not showed up for work. I felt that this was strange because supposedly, he was away doing a training that they sent him on.

This phone call sent me on a quest to seek the truth. But did I really want to know what he was hiding? Was I prepared to know the answer to the questions swimming around in my head. Why wasn't I enough for him? Why was he going to see other women on the side?

Why
Wasn't I all you ever wanted?
You have me but yet you don't want me.
You want the illusion of possession.
You want to hold me on your arm.
Like a trophy,

You sit me there on the shelf to collect dust
While you go about
Seeking whom you may devour,
You are a snake,
A liar,
A cheat...
But I love you.
And I wonder why?
What does she have between her thighs that makes you run to
her?
Am I not enough?
Have I not done all I could do to please you?
But yet you are not satisfied.
Your thirst is not quenched
And I am drowning in my tears
Asking myself
WHY?

Once again rejected.
Once again disrespected.
You laugh and think it's a joke.
You fill my head with lies.
You torture me with the past
As I scream out to be heard,
But no one hears.
No one sees the tears I cry at night
As I ask myself
WHY?

I looked through his phone bills and even called a few of these women. Oh yes there was one in Florida and one in Michigan and neither of them new of me or each other. He hid them all from me. But his lies were coming to an end.

As the phone rang, I was holding plane tickets in my hand that he foolishly sent to our address. I answered the phone and it was him telling me he was in jail.

In jail! What a lie! I let him know that I knew all about his trip to see the white chick in Florida. I let him know that I talked to her and that his lie was found out!

Tag!

I got you now. His little lie was found out. I just had wished I had headed the warning signs before I said I do.

It was December. We had gotten married in June. Just 6 months of marriage and I was living in a nightmare. I had already felt the pain of infidelity. I was reliving the past of all the men who left or cheated on me.

Not now! Not this time.
He tried to speak to me from the other line.

"I am in Jail." He kept saying but I couldn't hear him for the thoughts swimming around in my head.
"I am not on my way to the airport to go to Florida, I am in Jail" He kept repeating.
In jail? How could this be? What had he done?

He confessed of the lies and asked for my forgiveness but his time was running out for his call. He needed me to come down to court in the morning.

Chapter 22

The Second Time's a Charm?

The second time was supposed to be a charm.

Life was supposed to be better now. I had Christ in my life.
He was supposed to make all things new. He could fix
anything.
Why couldn't He fix my marriage?
Why couldn't He fix my life?
Why was my new husband in jail?
Why didn't he love me like he said?
He said he waited all his life to have me back and this is how
he treats me?

So many questions...
I try but it is not good enough
An never ending cycle
of trying to please one or another..
desiring to do what I am incapable of doing...
not having what I want to give..
do I shy back...??
shrinking into self..
Do I cry over and over again?
yet things still remain the same.
Do I lift my head
knowing that no matter what
I will never please them..
and you..
and him ..
and her..
no matter how I try.
It is impossible..

The more you give, the more they want...
I have no more to give...
so I run to You...
replenish my soul
fill me up Lord..
hide me...
Make me whole.
as they ask for more...
what would I not give?...
but I have nothing left..
You gave your all for me..
and so why should I worry
about them ...
and you..
and him..
and her...
the human side of me cares..
But My spirit cries out..
Enough!!!!

My souls cries out
WHY!!!??
and my body cringes at the thought
of having to carry this mess around..
"Stop!"
The torment of the mind..
reminding me of past failures...
"Stop!"
The whispering of the enemy...
telling me that I can never win...

"Be still!"
and Know that He is my only true HOPE!!!
My way out of no way...
when life seems hard...

He says take My Yoke
for it is easy and it is light..
I have carried this baggage for far too long..
I try.. I fail..
I try.. I fail..
I try.. I WIN...
It is not in failing..
but in the endurance to get back up again..
It is not in the despair..
but in overcoming the pain...
Victory is never being defeated...
even when you want to give up..

And everything within me wanted to give up. I began to drink myself to sleep to numb the pain. All I wanted to do was sleep because being awake only reminded me of what I didn't have that I longed to have. Part of me held on. My faith in God kept me going. The other half wondered why He hadn't rescued me from my life.

I was now faced with the idea of divorce number two. The things I greatly feared was upon me again as I had made an inward vow to never divorce because of what it had done to me. Perhaps if we ran away from it all, and started a new life. Perhaps things would be different.

Chapter 23

The Grass is not always Greener

I had to find a way of escape. I had to get away from the eyes of all those who looked on and shook their head as I decided to stay with my new husband. Against my better judgement I stayed. I wanted to fix my marriage. I didn't want to be a failure again.

After a heated argument and fist fight between my ex and my new husband over the treatment of the kids.

Kids? Oh yeah! I had kids, 4 to be exact but my life was so consumed with trying to find love that I forgot all about them. I took care of them. I fed them. I clothed them but I only nurtured and nursed my own wounds. I was too wounded to be there for them.

Oh don't get me wrong I loved and still love them with all my heart, but with everything that was going on in my life, and with my own wounded soul, I was like a BIG kid trying to raise a bunch of little ones.

I figured if I gave the kids to their father or someone, my life would be easier so after the "fight" their father insisted on taking them and I let them go. The only problem with them going to live with him was that he didn't end up taking them. He dropped them off at my mother's house. At the time I was so upset that he didn't take care of his own responsibility that I refused to come and get them from my mother's house. He had taken hem, he didn't like my new husband and neither did the kids. I had raised them by myself and HE should not have passed them off on my mother. I told my mom to call their father to pick them up.

I figured that now I could concentrate on my relationship with my new husband and not have to deal with my ex or my kids getting in the way. The only child I brought with me was the baby who was now almost three. He was easy to deal with because he didn't have any loyalties to his father. He wasn't revolting against me like I thought the big kids were doing because they wanted their dad and not my new husband to be in their life. He even started calling my new husband "Daddy".

I thought that moving to Hartford would give us a new start. I thought that not having the kids in the way would help strengthen our bond as husband and wife but… it didn't.

Finding work after being in jail for 8 months was hard. Depression set in as I went out to find a job and provide for my family.

My husband, well, he played video games all day and as I soon found out, talked to his "friends" on the phone and computer still.

Something had to give and I found out that the grass was not always greener on the other side. But how do I get back? How do I erase the pain I caused over time to myself and my children? How do I face my mother after abandoning her and my children? How do I return to Bridgeport and face the many fingers of disapproval? Once again I was faced with hiding from the truth.

After 3 months of being in Hartford, I got my children back. We all lived in the two bedroom 3rd floor apartment. This put a major strain on my marriage because my "husband" never wanted to be the kids stepfather. He just wanted me. He actually resented me even having the children because he constantly reminded me of the fact that I killed his baby back when I was 16.

The landlord disapproved of all 6 of us living in the 2 bedroom apartment but I had to have my children back with me. I received complaints constantly about the running and playing. The landlords complained about the amount of water being used. Any and every reason they could find.. They complained.

We were evicted. We were out on the streets with nowhere to go. We packed the car with everything that would fit. Moved the rest of our belongings into storage and roamed the streets, driving around trying to figure out where we would go next. As night grew near, we finally decided that the only option was to head to the local shelter. A shelter! A place where I never believed I would ever have been.

My husband drove us into the lot. I went in with my kids and filled out the necessary paperwork. Shame and despair filled my heart as tears streamed down my check. I returned to the car with the news of our accommodations only to have my husband inform me that he was going to a "friends house".

How could he leave us? We were supposed to be in THIS together, for better and for worse. And this was definitely the worst! I was homeless because of him! He put me and my kids in this circumstance and now he was leaving me?

I called the only friends I knew he had in Hartford but they said they hadn't heard from him. I found comfort in having a place to sleep, but why here? Why was I here? I had a bachelors, I wasn't dumb. Or was I? A mutual friend convinced me that I needed to move on and do for myself and my 4 kids. He told me that I needed to go back to school, finish getting my teacher's certificate and do *me*. Half of me heard his words as the other half longed to have my husband return and rescue me from this place.

As I looked around I saw women banding together to take care of their children. They were laughing and happy. I often wondered how they could be HAPPY in this place? Rows of beds lined the room we stayed in. Women talked about their lives and how they got to this place of homelessness. They shared of the love and hope they felt from God. I felt ashamed as I was supposed to be a Believer, but in my heart I felt that God had abandoned me. I prayed and cried myself to sleep.

Lord,
take this pain away
the feelings of
rejection
alienation
humiliation
leading to depression
Take away the sorrow...
the tears
the fears
allow me to rest in Your arms...
for I am
~tired of thinking
~tired of wishing
~tired of hoping
for things
that never seem to come true
prayers left unanswered...

give me the patience to
WAIT...
~but how long?
take the pain away...
I don't want to feel it anymore.
I paint on a smile
to hide the tears
and laugh when I want to cry.
Give me the strength to go on...
take the pain away...
what more could I say...
what more could I do...
I did all I could...
Do I not have
~needs?
~desires?
~dreams?.
~hopes?

Let them align with YOURS..
for my own surely fail...
and I am tired of trying
~take the pain away...

I woke up the next morning with a phone call from my husband who had found a place for us to go. He asked his sister if we could live with her.

From there we roamed from place to place. We lived at my mother's, my best friends, and his sister's trying to make ends meet and still hold onto what was left of our marriage. I tired to keep the faith but it was often difficult, as I looked at the current circumstances and wondered if it would ever get any better.

Chapter 24

Escaping Truth

Truth was I was not happy. I was living a lie. My second marriage was failing and there seemed to be nothing I could do about it.

He continued to see other women behind my back. I was hurt and searching for comfort. I desired to be loved, even at the expense of being deceitful.

One evening after an argument, I went for a ride. Dancing had always been a way to let out my frustrations with life, aside from writing. I ended up at a club I had frequented in the past and there he was sitting there smiling at me. I tried not to look at him but he captured my eye. He had my full attention as he asked me for my name and number. I could not resist the temptation. It felt good to be looked at with desire; something I wasn't getting at home. We started talking to each other on the phone. Talking turned into meeting and meeting well.. turned into sex. I justified my actions, saying that I was only doing what was done to me. If he could do it, why couldn't I? Didn't I deserve to have someone desire me?

He was charming, intriguing, and sexy.
He smiled and my heart melted.
With each kiss...
With each touch...
His eyes reached deep within my soul
calling out to me.
I had to have him.
He was my teddy bear.

My sexy chocolate.
Forbidden
But Mine,
Just for the asking.
Whatever I desired
He was at my beck and call
Until guilt set in
And I had to let him go...

Even though I was falling for him, I knew what I was doing was wrong. Although it felt so right. He begged me to leave my husband and be with him. I fought inwardly, because I had always wanted someone who truly loved me. I longed to be loved even if it was wrong. He was charming. We often spent late afternoons and evenings just talking. He listened to me which is more than I could say about my husband. I loved and craved the attention. I would sneak off, making up any excuse just to see him. It was easy to escape because my husband was preoccupied with his other women so he never noticed the smile on my face when I returned.

With every kiss, with every touch my conscience would not allow me to fully enjoy this new found love. I knew in my heart that it was wrong but it felt so good. He confessed his love but I couldn't stay. So I pushed him away.

Sometimes I wonder what would have become of us, if I had stayed.

Chapter 25

Failed Again

I was left with yet another decision. Should I stay and endure the pain of being with someone who did not love me? Or should I leave; failing again in the arena of marriage. The idea of being divorced twice made my stomach turn. Deep down I wanted to be loved. My heart broke. I began to lose all hope and fell into a state of depression. Why didn't anyone love me? I would often ask as voices in my head reminded me of my past.

"Your dad left you, why would anyone love you?
You killed his baby!
You're bad.
Everyone is against you.
No One loves you.
You are better off DEAD!
You are Better OFF
DEAD!"

I am better off dead.

No one would notice or care if I were gone. Once again I became preoccupied with the idea of drifting off into a deep sleep and never waking. The thoughts consumed me until one day during an argument with my husband, I started popping pills right in front of him, screaming and crying.

I am not sure if I really wanted to die. I just didn't want to live with the pain and the thoughts that I had deep inside. I wanted the pain to stop. I wanted the lies to stop. But how?

Was death really the answer? I asked myself as I sat in the padded room they placed me in at the hospital. It all was a fog as people came in asking me random questions. Tears streaming down my face, I see a trace of a man. As he drew closer, and held me, he whispered I love you in my ear. It was a familiar voice. When I looked at the face, I realized that it was my dad. Who had called him? And why was he here? Mixed emotions filled my mind. Should I embrace the idea that he really loved me or was this all a plot to get me to snap out of this state of depression. No one understands my complicated mind. Sometimes I wonder if God can even hear me, but I held onto faith in the midst of failure.

Pondering things I should not.
Trying to undo what was said,
the voice inside my head.
The things I received in my heart.
Uprooting the damage of the past.
Erasing the memories.
The thoughts of inadequacies
seemed to be my greatest enemy.
Seeds sown.
Echos in my mind.
A voice heard from within.
Wash away the stains.
Take away the pains.
Within this complicated mind.

What I choose to do affects my future.
Emotions lying dormant rise.
Coming against what I know to be true.
Memories trapped
as Love guards me
protecting me from

Myself.
You lift me Lord.
Above this complicated mind.
Being renewed daily.
Prune away those things which remind me of who I was.
The things once said.
Feelings trapped within.
Give me the strength, Lord.
As I reach out to you.
Clinging to your Mighty Hand.
For I am weak
It is the Word that speaks...
That gives me hope
for a brighter tomorrow...
My soul cries out
As Your Spirit lifts me
For I can not do this on my own
To overcome this complicated mind...
Renewing it to You...
And who you have called me to be
Fill me Lord,
and set me free
Erase the words sown
In the midst of battle
I hear You say...
That You made me...
This Way

The things I see that are wrong..
He will make them right
For I could never achieve what you have for me,
without Him...

Just Trust
Believe with all my heart...
That He will bring me to the point
of Victory
over this
Complicated Mind...

My mother convinced them to release me from the hospital. I went home with her. My husband seemed to have drifted off into the sunset. He called a few times here and there but it was over. Marriage #2 failed and now I was left alone to continue on this journey to live a life I never wanted to live.

Once again I was a single mother, raising four kids on my own. Thank God for my mother who hung in there no matter what. But I had to figure this out on my own. I had to make it. But How?

Chapter 26

Rejected By God?

I turned to the church once more seeking answers. I figured if I got counseling for these issues, everything would be okay. But I was sadly mistaken. The pastors confirmed my fears, and pointed fingers at me as if I were *bad* for contemplating suicide. They accused me of shaming them as pastors, stating what if someone at the hospital recognized me and my affiliation with their church it would have put a damper on the ministry.

How could I be saved and have such thoughts. They felt like it was a slap in their face that I would ever think of such a thing.

Suicide?

Depression?

They stripped me of my titles. Yes, I had a few titles in church and I was a regular attender. Through all of these struggles I attended church faithfully. I was a Born Again Christian, tongue talking, bible toting Christian.

I was one of the heads of the children's ministry. I was in the choir. I was newly appointed as the Drama Team Director. How dare I have thoughts of inadequacy? How dare I attempt to take my life? As a member of their church? How dare I be contemplating divorce.

Fingers of accusation were pointed at me on every side. Did God really love me, especially now that my life was a mess? Could He love me now that I had committed adultery, which I dared not divulge? Were these pastors right? Did I shame them and God by my actions. Would I ever be forgiven?

The enemy tried to make me feel like God didn't love me anymore. After all how could He? I had a sinful nature, I was a mess. My life was in a shamble even though I professed to know God but my actions dictated a life of defeat. Was God rejecting me? Was God punishing me for all the wrong I had done in the past?

I started to shy away from God. Turning inwardly, I started to take in all the words of rejection. I began to hate myself even more than I had before because it was one thing to have people turn their back on me but God? Did God turn his back on me too?

I try ...
but it is not good enough.
An never ending cycle
of trying to please one or another..
desiring to do
what I am incapable of doing...
not having what I want to give..
Do I shy back...??
shrinking into self..

Do I cry over and over again..
yet remain the same..
or do I lift my head
knowing...
that no matter what
I will never please them..

Or you..
Or him ..
Nor her..
no matter how I try..
it is impossible..
The more you give..
the more they want...
I have no more to give...
so I run
to You...
replenish my soul
fill me up Lord..
hide me...
They ask for more...
what would I not give...
but I have not...
Yet You gave Your all for me..
and so why should I worry about
them ...
or you..
or him..
or her...
the human side of me cares..
as My spirit cries out..
Enough!!!!
My souls cries out
WHY!!!??
and my body cringes at the thought
of having to carry this mess around..
Stop!
The torment of the mind..
reminding me of past failures...

Stop!
The whispering of the enemy...

telling me that I can never win...
Be still!
and Know that He is my only true HOPE!!!
My way out of no way...
when life seems hard...
He says take My Yoke
for it is easy and it is light..
I have carried this baggage for far too long..
I try.. I fail..
I try.. I fail..
I try.. I WIN...
It is not in failing..
but in the endurance to get back up again..
It is not in the despair..
but in overcoming the pain...
Victory is
never being defeated...
even when you want to give up..

And give up is what I did. Not on God but I was on the loose again. Searching and seeking. Trying to hide the pains deep inside I fled from one church to another again. In search of healing.

Chapter 27

A Place of Restoration

This House shall be called
a Place a Restoration
A place where the broken Hearts made whole
Healing waters flow
as Mercy abides here
My Spirit abides here
Saith the Lord.

The words of this song rang true in my heart. As I listened to this song I felt the LOVE of God pour over me. Never before had I felt so free to be me. Not the person that others wanted me to be or even feeling the shame of not living up to God's standards but a new freedom of acceptance even with all my junk. He loves me.

The Bishop ministered to my soul, preaching a message of a loving God. So many times I had heard the messages of God but felt condemned for not being perfect. But time God had led me to a place where I felt safe. I still hid behind the walls I had built over time but slowly, brick by brick, I began to tear down the wall.

Healing is a process.
A Journey of discovery
of who you are
And who you long to be.
No more playing this game
Of Hide and Seek.
I am on this Journey Called Life.

Seeking God
In order to Find
The REAL ME.
Desiring to be truly free.
No more chains of misery
I am loosed to be
Authentically me.
Life is a Journey
Filed with ups and downs.
But I am learning each day
To look in the mirror and like what I see
As I walk towards Victory
One Day at A Time.

Made in the USA
Columbia, SC
11 December 2018